When Languag Left Me

Post-Stroke Poems

More kind words
for *When Language Left Me*

———————————— ◆ ————————————

"In *When Language Left Me*, Farzana Marie grapples with the effects of a massive stroke—an event that split her life into a before and an after. Word by word, poem by poem, this powerful volume charts her way forward, as she crafts a lyrical path of courage, transformation, hope, and resilience."

-Juhi Bansal, award-winning Composer, Conductor, and Teacher

"Farzana's poetry captures poignantly the initial trauma and daily struggles of life with aphasia. Although aphasia is different for everyone, I believe many people living with aphasia will nod in recognition as they read or listen to these poems. And for those unfamiliar with aphasia, it gives a rare and powerful glimpse into what it is like to lose language."

-Fabi Hirsch Kruse, PhD, CCC-SLP
Co-Founder: Friends of Aphasia

"Farzana Marie illuminates obstacles as muses as she allows us insight into her suddenly alien identity. *When Language Left Me* maintains a steady arc towards a constantly shifting horizon. Along the way, Farzana cedes time and space to rest and perspective—'Sleep no longer the enemy…'—as she dreams a new life into being. These poems bring the poet and the reader together, on our shared plain of humanity, to each examine and explore our identity, our fragility, our power, and the possibilities to be found within ourselves."

-PW Covington, New Mexico Beat Poet Laureate

"After a stroke in Afghanistan nearly erased her—and her treasured languages—Farzana Marie writes herself back—word by word—with humor, wonder, and a relentless spirit that turns loss into beauty, meaning, and, ultimately, transcendence."

-Nassim Assefi, MD, Novelist, Creative Curator, and Civic Activist

When Language Left Me

Farzana Marie

Abandoned Mine
Albuquerque, NM

Published by *Abandoned Mine*, a poetry press.

ISBN: 979-8-218-87419-3

For information about discounts on bulk orders, please contact
the editors of *Abandoned Mine* at: poetry@abandonedmine.org

For people with aphasia
(*Have hope!*)

Also by Farzana Marie:

Poetry Chapbook

Letters to War and Lethe

Poetry Translation

Load Poems Like Guns:
Women's Poetry from Herat, Afghanistan

Non-Fiction

Hearts for Sale: A Buyer's Guide
to Winning in Afghanistan

Contents

Foreword

It's hard to describe what it feels like to have aphasia.

That's not only because you're reaching for words that no longer come easily to you. It's not only because you spend so much time inside your mind, trying to force yourself to shape the words you want to say, often without much luck.

It's ultimately because it's such a unique experience. Every person with aphasia experiences it differently. Everyone has individual, private battles with their own words, and everyone has their own support system to help them.

But Farzana's book of poetry, *When Language Left Me*, captures it.

I've had aphasia since January 2011, when I was shot in the head by someone who wanted to assassinate me. I was representing Arizona's 8th District in Congress at the time, and I was hosting a constituent event at a local grocery store. Six people died, and 13 more were injured—including me. I wasn't supposed to survive.

But I did. When I woke up six days later, I was surrounded by friends and family. I felt safe. Until I tried to speak.

When you can't get words out, your first instinct is often to use simpler words to convey your point. Surely, that must be easier for your tongue to pronounce. But when that doesn't work, what do you do? How do you explain your thoughts or express your feelings? How do you tell the people you know you love them?

Farzana's poems speak straight to the heart. They wrap around your soul.

Before her stroke, Farzana spoke six languages. She worked with locals in Afghanistan to ease tensions and connect with the communities. She was getting her PhD in Afghan women's poetry. Words and language were her oxygen.

Now, like many of us with aphasia, she can't speak the way she used to. She can't read the way she used to. Her mastery of so many languages isn't the same.

When you experience a life-changing moment like this, the future you planned is irrevocably altered. You can't return to the life you once lived—but you can shape your future. You can choose what you want to do with your days, who you want to spend your time with. And every day, Farzana boldly, courageously, and faithfully chooses to relearn what she had lost.

Farzana is an inspiration to many with aphasia. We are not on an easy journey—we face setbacks and "obstinate obstacles" every day. But she wakes up and puts one foot in front of the other. She says one word after another. She finds the words she needs, she creates powerful art, and she leads with love. This book is a beautiful journey, and I hope you enjoy it as much as I did.

-former Congresswoman Gabrielle Giffords

I. Lifescare

This Bench, Part One

This bench:
simple, wooden, long.
Ordinary.

I walked by it
every day.

I Skyped with my sister,
in my dorm,
on the base,
in Kabul,
Afghanistan.

I was happy.

I walked the hall
passing the makeshift crate
of free stuff:
magazines, books, DVDs,
ramen, oatmeal, hot cocoa,
sanitary necessities, and
thoughtful, innocent cards from
US elementary school kids.

I felt cared for
as I stepped outside.

Normally at night
I would work on my dissertation:

Sharp-Edged Verse in 21st Century Afghanistan:

From the Silence and War to the Wide Open Page,
An Analysis of Socio-Political Dimensions in Women's Poetry.

But tonight, Friday,
I would visit with my friends.

But tonight, something was off.
I felt...a never-before feeling.
I grabbed the bench and sat down.

I remember
I fall

     and blackout.

I remember
that day

     and that's all I remember.

Extraterrestre

Kabul (Afghanistan)

I have fallen.

I'm divided.

Two people—
one of me is nearby,
over there,
suspended.

And the other me,
what's happened to her?

Dizzy?   *No, not dizzy.*
Spinning?   *No, not spinning.*

             Overpowered!

I watched in horror
as the *extraterrestre*
stole all my controls.

My body has become an alien to me,
and rendered me

        comatose.

        Alteredtime.

begun: 2016
completed: 2025

Error

The corpse is still.

(I'm still here)

The dividing by zero
undefined
can't compute something
from nothing.

Can't taste
can't feel
can't hear
can't speak
my brain
shuts down.

Error

       Error

            Error

                Error

begun: 2016
completed: 2025

Too Late

for Timur

Untold hours
unconscious.

My clothes wet
with sweat and urine.
Vomit. Excrement.

Hair matted
to my face.

My boss and friend, Timur,
doesn't recognize me.

Kabul Base has tiny clinic.
Doctor there thinks
overdose?

Timur scoffs.
*I know this woman.
She didn't overdose.*

Medics carry my body to
the Black Hawk helicopter,
transport me to hospital
at Bagram Air Base.
Tests reveal stroke.

Good news:
have it—tPA—
brain saver medicine
(maybe life saver).

But:
Too late, cautiously says Doctor,
out of the four-hour window.
Timur make the decision:

    High-risk medication?
     or
    High-risk no medication?

Impossible to choose.
He decides no medication.

I survived.

But:
My language is

       gone.

1-min

Bagram Air Base (Afghanistan)

blip
where are me?

incapacitated

bagram
timur
rabbi?

what?
what?
¿que?
bale?

serious.

sick.

transport...

ohh

¿¿pasaporte??

coma again

begun: 2016
completed: 2020

Panic

Hospital, Dubai (UAE)

Pain
woke me up.

Many nurses
black vultures
on a carcass

on me

all over my body
poke, prod,
OUCH
Hey—I am alive
STOP!

Thrash

I thought
       I am strong
but
I am weak.

Nurses tied me
      down
to the bed.

I am helpless.
I panicked.

Blacked out

again.

begun: 2016
completed: 2020

BEEP

for Emily

Silence.

My silence (coma).

But in the room
relentless noise:

       BEEP... BEEP...

           BEEP... BEEP...

               BEEP... BEEP...

Coming to.

A solitary nurse hovers.
Behind her, a familiar face.

I *know* her.

My sister?

Don't know her name.

Sink
into sleep
again.

She fights—
my sister—
for me.

Drop everything,
travel to me.

Sleepless nights. BEEP...

Worry. BEEP...

Prayer. BEEP...

Her chin is firm.
Her eyes are fire.

What does it take to move the world?

Numb

Hospital, Abu Dhabi (UAE)

Stun
shock
can't move

     arm-branch
     leg-wooden
     torso-trunk
     face-putty

Play-Doh
disembodied
right hangs
dead weight

     My brain is swollen

     slooooooowed down

     reassemble synapses
     discombobulated.

begun: 2016
completed: 2020

Lifescare

Hospital, Phoenix (USA)

My parents
meet me.
I can't talk,
can't write.

Tried drawing
and pantomime but...
How do I say,

I long to be home.

Remembering my dad
slowly walking with me
in the Phoenix hospital.
Who were we now together?
Once we shared a tight bond.
We loved acting, languages,
we were spontaneous with each other,
we loved the world in the same way.
He was always so proud of me.
The music of our punning has changed;
so has the duet.
He was stunned and devastated to see me
and me, who was I then to him?
Who was I then to me?

I long to be home.

Remembering my mom
shaving my armpits.
No words—
only mother's comfort and love.
I gravitate to my mom right away.
She masks her shock with
grace.

I long to be home.

Remembering my sister, Emily,
in the hospital,
sleeping by my side.
She traveled to Dubai.
Always devoted.
Emily translates me
(I didn't know it at the time),
my ally.

I long to be home.

Remembering playing chess.
I beat the male nurse.
No words.
He—astonished.
Me,

I long to be home.

Remembering the physical therapist.
We went to the tiny grass—
not the park—just patch of green grass.
She throws the Frisbee.
My right hand can't play;
too limp.
My left hand takes charge.
Now I am ambidextrous.
Me?
I am clumsy.

I long to be home.

Remembering my speech therapist.
Indescribably
Painful.
Basic things.
Recalling 50/50.
Tedious.
Painfully
Exhausting.
And I am so sad and angry.
Speech therapist with endless questions:

> *Are paint and syrup used to take a bath in?*
> no/yes
> (My mind says, "*Funny! Perhaps?*")

> *Can pigs walk on two feet?*
> no/yes
> (My mind says, "*Piglet can walk and talk on two legs!*")

My mind still amuses me.

Are band-aids used for healing?
no/yes

No?
Or Yes?

I long to be home.

Remembering my younger brother, Eric.
He joined my speech therapy sessions
to keep me company.
How he hid beneath his hoodie
a man-boy struggling to hide.
I know he cries.
How could he bear such heaviness?
Our bond of love, so strong,
sharing hiking, storytelling, music,
just hanging with each other—happiness...

now in silence.

I long to be home.

I long to be

I long

18

Vanished. Submerged. Sunk.

My tongue
can't produce
the sounds.

Español?
      Nope.
Dari?
      Nope.
Kazakh?
      Nope.
Russian?
      Nope.
Arabic?
      Nope.

English??!

No.

noooooooo.

no...

My beloved languages
                            are gone.

Once vibrant and hot conversation
flowed.

Now
vanished—
      submerged—

sunk.

And I am frozen,
immobile,
bound to haunting stillness.

Without language.

No words for colors
or numbers
          or days
                    or foods.
No prepositions or articles.
No words for people's names.
No words for feelings.
No questions.
No A B C.

Start again.
Steel my mind.

In the rubble that stroke left behind,
          I search,
          I dig for my lost treasures,
my language,
my own work,
sacred antiquity—
lost.

And I sleep.

My Lot

I am walking,
slowly.
I am numb
right side:
my foot,
my leg,
my hand,
my shoulder,
my cheek.

Still,
I am walking.
Grateful.

But:
no speech.
Pathetically slow.
Breath by breath.
Every day.
Week by week.
Month by month.
Year by year.
Now a decade. (*A decade!*)
So slow.

It is like
drowning?
underground
but still seeing
people walking by
speaking—so effortlessly!

I. Am. Envious.

Please, God.

I accept my lot.

Not true.
I *recognize* my lot.
The black hole in my brain.

But I fight.
Rewire my brain.
For the rest of my life.

I learning again:
my mother tongue
like a foreign language.
Strangers—
so many strangers—ask:
What country are you from?

Wire by wire by wire.

But don't worry,
dear reader,
and don't pity me.

I have grit.
I pick myself up.

I adapt
to this new, atypical culture.

I change.

Rewire.

Recognize my lot
as language
                    electrician.

NO

for Rachel Owen

Rach traveled to my parents' home,
Chandler, Arizona,
one month after my stroke,
on my birthday, I am 32.
It's autumn and hot.

She redeployed home.
She was afraid that
her dear friend, me,
had changed,
no longer the same.
She was worried.

I open the door to greet,
my dearest friend.

Embrace.
Lock eyes.

Nearly speechless.
I have just a few words:
"Camel." "Hi." "No."
Maybe "Yes."

Rach doesn't worry
ever.
But today she is worried.

It's getting dark.

I want to go to the park.

I am determined to go to the park.
But how do I say it?

I can't say
        park

I can't say
        Frisbee

"No," is my park.

"No," is my Frisbee.

"No," is my go:

I march to the park.

Rach smiles.

Still here.
My friend,
still here.

Rach understands my no.

Tongue

Sounds.
Such lovely sounds.

The feel of sounds
that rolls around my tongue,
like peppermints.

The touch
soft like
Persian cashmere.

I will
my tongue:
      Tongue, perform!

I gently
touch my tongue.

I call out to
my tongue.

I beseech
my tongue.

I command
my tongue.

Sometimes *Yes*.
Sometimes *No*.

But I keep at it.

I miss you, Tongue.

Crayons-Canoe

Tucson, Arizona

A light, narrow boat ~

created colors:

      of raw sienna,

      of burnt orange,

      of cadet blue.

Pointed with no keel,

propelled with no paddles

      and

            bitter-sweet.

begun: 18 September 2016
completed: 6 October 2016

One Bee

frantic

colliding with the window

pane.

Trapped.

The swarm, oblivious, busy

with pink

Queen Wreath Vine.

begun: October 2016
completed: November 2016

Aphasia Skeleton*

Wings spread,
absent sinew

beak open,
silent cry

wounded foot
taking step

pink bone
weirding language

short hall
a long way to go.

begun and completed: May 2017

*This is an ekphrastic poem, written in response to the image of a
skeleton of a large bird in mid-step in the foreground of a
darkened hallway.

30

Blank

for Nick V.K.

My hands flutter as I pick
them from the air:
images and words floating.
I grab for them
and try to puzzle fit.
One sentence.
I can't compose one sentence.
Not one sentence.
Not "not one *beautiful* sentence."
Just no sentence
       at all.

Words are chipped
     f r a g m—

I try to put them together
but the words go sideways.

But where the words were, there are blank blank

heart	blank	blank	ache	blank	blank
blank	crying	out	blank	blank	frustrate
blank	mmm	blank	blank	blank	blank
grief	blank	blank	blank	grief	blank
blank	blank	blank	blank	blank	longing...

Something disappeared. Missing.

     It's like the books
     are
     blank the library.

The birds blank
the trees.

begun: 2018
completed: 2023

Walking the *Bosque*

Albuquerque, New Mexico

I am walking the *bosque*.
I sit in the trees
and listen closely.
Rustling cottonwood leaves.

My grief
sleeps and awakens:
porcupines in the trees.

My grief—
little orange hawkweed—
flowers and fades
on my landscape.

It surrounds me
        envelops me.

My grief buzzes
a million flies
in my ear.

Stop it.
STOP IT.

The buzzing
won't quit.

I listen to
throaty croaking cranes
in the Rio Grande.

Their song delights me.

My own croaking
does not delight me.

How do I delight in my self?

Trespassing

She is named Aphasia.
    Aphasics speak don't
    but all think   always
    frenetic   scramble   is
                        constant.

She is named Apraxia.
    Stifling.
    Choking.
    Voiceless.
    Helpless.

She is named Alexia.
    Desperate to read
    but can't.
    Desperate to translate
    but can't.
    Desperate to tell my story
    but can't.

Long running.
Long struggle.
Long grieving.
Long breath-taking time.

      Long silence.

Sleep

Where did my stroke come from?

Stress?
Not likely. I thrived on high-stress:
the challenges of the Air Force Academy,
volunteer year at an orphanage in Central Asia,
TedX talk, 26.2-mile Bataan Memorial Death March
(in boots and carrying a 35-lb. rucksack),
jumping out of airplanes, Afghanistan deployments...
Maybe.

Genetics?
A relative before me had a stroke. Left brain.
Young. Like me.
Maybe.

Sleep? Ohhhhh...
Big maybe.

Did my lost sleep from so many years ago
come back to find me?

I thought I didn't need sleep.
Defied the hours.
Time for sleep would be later—too many
important books to write.

I was defiant.
Arrogant.

The imperative now?

Surrender to exhaustion,
sleep no longer the enemy.

I befriend my sleep.

I dreamt
without aphasia
and with aphasia.

I am dreaming
about
tiny sprouts,
bright possibilities,
glimpse to visions.

I am dreaming
a new life.

II. Satin Repair

Unexpected

Tucson, Arizona

Mulberry Fire
  burned
  to the ground.
  Start over.
          Hole.

Barren—my backyard.
Brick by brick
  new soil
  nurture and watering
  new life.

I scoop from the ground—
curious—
I look up...
soft and sweet,
purple and white,
hidden and fat
and so ripe fruit.
          Tuut!*
I climb the ladder,
neighbor's tree
hanging over.
          Whole.

God left

                    a gift
                    a taste of Afghanistan.

Zenda bosheyn—
          May you be alive.

Tuut: "mulberry" in Dari (Persian)

Returning Independence

for Emily

Emily: my unexpected voice
and unexpected housemate.

No words to fully say *Thank you*
and *It's time to leave.*

Ready to be me again.

Tried to be gentle.

Please forgive my failing, Em.

Te amo para siempre.

40 years old

30: decade is gone.
It was tedious
like squeezing grapes
stomped
pressed
crushed
I won.
I won.
I am winning!

It was maddening.
That's why I stomped
pressed
crushed:
to be lucid.

To unjumble my brain.

Somehow I was overcome with love
love that bonded together
intimate friends and family
unswerving in their commitment.

I had no speech—
they kept talking anyway.

My brain abandoned me.
Not entirely.
Did my God abandon me?
Not entirely.
I have recognized my aphasia
to be my life condition.

Not entirely.

My stroke has left me incredulous.
How could this be my life?
The paradox continues.
I am fascinated by my brain
which has recalibrated.
I feel it.
My mind and I have joined up.
We are partners.

It's been eight long years.

Here, here!

Satin Repair

for Annika

Worked wood.
Annika's father loves the cracks.
Holzarbeiten ~

that's what shows its
Uniqueness.

Scars.

*Pain, missed opportunities, the hard labor of becoming
who we were or who we are meant to be.*

Excruciating.

I lit a candle for Advent,
round wood holder
Annika jan gave me in Kabul
three years after my stroke.

Gentle, light, silky
flowing words
fills the cracks.

Satin repair.

Imperfect.
Perfect.
Beautiful.

Bending the mending.

For Granted

Order drive-through
        for granted

Cards & letters
        for granted

Conversations
        for granted

Post-style earrings
        for granted

My bra
        for granted

Tying shoes
        for granted

Button on
or off
        for granted

Driving
        for granted

Pick up the phone—
for the appointment
for the bank
for the VA
for the kid's school
for the library...
Just chatting

for granted

Emergency call
my address
my phone
describe a situation
for granted

Make up the story
for granted

Singing
for granted

Reading
Reading poems
Reading children's books
Reading recipes (*Recipes!*)

All

for granted.

Limitations and Lamentations

I teach myself again
the days of the week,
my alphabet & numbers.
I quiz myself.
My grades are so-so.

Reading for necessity,
mundane:
like instructions: *how to construct the kitchen island,*
or *how to install the car seat covers,*
or *parent/teacher directions.*

I guess.
I try.
I imagine.
and finally
I text
"Help Me."

Afternoon, my daughter & I read
short books
and she says
"again."
I take a pause
and rest my brain.
Then I read again.
But evening fatigue sets in.
Daddy reads.

How to know anew
how to do the world
ordinary

and
extraordinary.

I am Flour

Tucson, Arizona

I am flour.

No... Flower

NOOO... I am sloan

Sigh.

I am SLOW!

Great. Winner!

Small triumph.

Apraxia meets

auto correct.

Rearranging the Tofu

On and on, every week,
building comical mini stories.
Like: "I went off on a tantrum..."
I mean "...on a tangent..."

See?

Unintentionally
lightening up the room.

Happens all the time:

Me:	I will go to the walrus!
Husband:	*Walgreens?*
Me:	Yes! Wal - greens!

Me:	Oh! You rearranged the tofu!
Neighbor:	*Oh! You mean futon?*
Me:	Ugh! Yes. I like it!

Me:	The color is irrigation.
Speech therapist:	*Irrigation?*
Me:	I mean ir - i - de - scent?
	Descent into the abyss??

Me:	Please, give me persimmon to play!
Friend:	*Permission?*
Me:	Yes. Exactly. Per - mi - ssion!

Me:	I need to chance my password!
Husband:	*Change?*
Me:	Ha ha. I need to change me.

Me:	What animal?
Young child:	*Prairie dog?*
Me:	Close! GoFundMe!
Young child:	*Huh?*
Me:	(Breathe.) Go - pher!

Me:	Care for a potsticker?
Nephew:	*You said potsticker?*
Me:	No. I meant pop - si - cle!
Nephew:	*OH! Yes, please!*

Me:	Help! Distinguish the fire in the oven!
Husband:	*OK! Extinguish?*
Me:	YES!

Me:	Honey! Apple cider!
Husband:	*Cool! Apple cider?*
Me:	Oh. No. Apple... App - e - ti - zer!

Me:	You are pressure!!
Daughter:	*Mmm?*
Husband (whisper):	*Precious.*
Me:	You are precious!

Me:	My muse is obstacle!
Poetry therapist:	*Mmm... Obstinate?*
Me:	Yes. My muse is ob - sti - net.
	Sometimes ob - sta - cle too!

Me:	You like your comfy scissors?
Niece:	*My comfy slippers?*
Me:	Yesss. Your comfy slippers!

Me:	We have a tomato warning!
Friend:	*Oh dear! Tomatoes?? You mean, tornado warning?*
Me:	Possible!! ;)

Me:	I like the coffee shop, Cutthroat!
Brother:	*What?*
Me:	I mean, Cutbow Coffee!
Brother:	*Ohh! Ha ha!*

Me:	There! I threw the rubber duckies, the crocodile, the turtle, the elephant, the starfish, and the apricot into the bathtub!
Daughter:	*Apricot, Mama??*
Me:	Hmm... Oc - to - pus!
Daughter:	*You got it, Mama! Bravo!*

High Tea

for Rev. Nan – Rhinebeck, New York

I walked in curious
preparing to sit down to high tea.

Soft-colored teacups (lavender, mint, lemon)
on white tablecloths.

I chose the brilliant lapis-colored one.

Berry-scones, still warm from the oven,
on tiered stands with rich creams and jams
and other treats.

Nan held a newfound appreciation
for simple pleasures, adorning
each table with wildflowers
she had handpicked: bluebell,
crimson bee balm, barren strawberry,
thimbleberry, firewheels, chicory.

Not long ago, Nan had been
very sick:
Food administered only by IV.
Drink administered only by IV.
Many surgeries.

She prayed to God
to be peacefully at rest and
no longer hurting

or to be alive and healed.

Doctor said permanent IV.
Dependent for life.

Lifelong?

People prayed.
And prayed.
And prayed.

After awhile, Nan could take small bites
and sips—could taste again.

She started baking scones again,
started having tea.

Now, years later, Nan can eat
and drink anything she wants.

Now, Nan prays for healing for me—

both of us knowing
that sometimes God heals

and sometimes
God doesn't heal.

Leadership

In the beginning,
front and center:

> Volunteering
> at school
> at church
> in the orphanage...
>
> And in my job
> (military officer)
> working against corruption
> and always seeking peace.
> Speaking in meetings
> and on TV.
> Speaking in Dari.

After stroke,
everything derailed.
No one following—or listening
(nothing to say).

Relegated to the back,
the end of the pack.

I'm an outsider,
a wallflower,
awkward.
Left out—

even of my own command.

This Bench, Part Two

for Aman

I finished
my defense dissertation—
a miracle: three years after my stroke.

Practiced the words for months.
All day, for months.
My brain hurt.

My reward?
First flight to Kabul.
Fall 2018.

No longer military.
Just a civilian who
understands Dari

but can't speak Dari.
                              Yet!
(Yet?)

At the base, I return to the bench:
Simple. Wooden. Long.
Ordinary.

Still here.

Run & Bouquet

for Aman & Wahid

Dubai hospital.

Timur and Em wonder:
  Where is the neurologist?
  Where is the translator?

Insurance issue? Politics?

  Why is no one helping her!?!?

Research and phone calls.
Better care in Abu Dhabi,
40 miles away.

But how to steal a comatose body?

The checklist:

☑ $20,000

☐ Guns

☑ Ambulance

☑ Driver

☑ Brave accomplices

The four bandits
Timur, Em, Aman, Wahid
secure the vehicles,
travel in the getaway car,

close behind the screeches
of the speeding ambulance.

Lawless manoeuvre, non-negotiable.

The patient is safely delivered.

Afghan friends
so dear to me—
so caring and gentle—
visit me,
but I don't remember.

I do remember the bouquet.
Garish yet stunning,
a vibrancy so strange.
Blue flowers.

It would be years
before I would see Aman again,
traveling in Kabul
in search of...what?

Friends?
My fall?
My grief?
My Dari?

Where is my missing me?

We sit in the quiet of a Kabul restaurant
and brainstorm.

Everything is possible in Kabul.
Difficult but possible.

Aman jan scribbles, then holds up
the plastic plate:
"Farzana Marie Stroke Rehabilitation Center"

Is this possible?
Difficult.
But possible.

We will build a healing clinic
together.

Thrive, Survivor

Words are such small things, like confetti in the brain,
and yet they color and clarify everything.

-Diane Ackerman, *One Hundred Names for Love: A Memoir*

Imagination is
handcrafted,
my house: the sun-filled loft,
the teal and royal blue window nook,
the balcony rocking-chair,
fluidly
      with
           words.

No warning, like a tornado ripping through:
my poetry,
my books,
my translations—
gone.
(Words my identity.)

Plagues me.
Blank page.

Fresh start
handcrafted,
my new yurt:
kilim, threshold,
korpeshes,
round high lens,
outside my garden:
Afghan apricot trees,
red hummingbird feeder,
kaleidoscope flowers,

and a rope hammock.

Painstaking
        with
                Words.

What if

1.

What if
I break out—
      like a gale
despacito
learning a new way to breathe
lining new synapses
in my brain.

2.

What if
I storm the castle
filled
      with rusted instruments
      with stranded musicians.
Fighting to liberate
radical notes and uncover phrases
from a royal blue viola
which vibrates and awakens.

3.

What if
I devour
      juicy orange roughy
and spicy mango pie.
I am craving.
Not satisfied with a single dandelion

I yearn for a whole field
to wish
tantalizing words to return.

4.

What if
I spelunk, scuba dive
        digging for tiny books
golden crinkling pages.
I am immersed in new waters
I back roll
into my subconscious.

5.

What if
I unmask
        the gorgeous paint
to reveal the stark and misshapen statue.
I am bold
poised and unruffled.

My Flamenco Skirt

Syncopated movement.

Sharp.

Tight.

Panache!

Flair!

> *Look at her.*
> *See her.*
> *Listen to her—feel!—her dance.*
> *There you will find her story.*

The skirt is made of heavy fabric,
mostly red, mostly black,
with ruffled hemline
and often a polka dot design:
lunares—little moons—mysterious,
which carry the nomadic legacy
of the Roma people.

My flamenco skirt is lapis lazuli
filled with
holes of light,
resembling polka dots,
large and tiny.
Unsettling.

The artist has longings—
trapped—
can't get out.

Can she access what she cannot give voice to?

I am practicing my wrists
round and round,
over and over—
like Kazakh dance—
two wrists together.

Her body discovers
through movement
how to express her primal longings.

I imagine
soon an atmospheric
choreography.

My feet:

                golpe

tacón

                tacón

golpe

                tacón

tacón

                golpe

             golpe

tacón

             tacón

golpe

             tacón

tacón

             golpe

             golpe

tacón

             tacón

golpe

             tacón

tacón

             golpe

             golpe x2

tacón

             tacón

golpe x2

             tacón

tacón

             golpe

golpe

             golpe

golpe

¡Olé!

My whole body
responds to my grief:

swirling,
whirling.

¡Cante!

¡Cante!

¡Cante!

Take me to my forgotten legacy,
where I moved in the world between worlds,
touched by mystery.

Golpe and Lullaby

por Amalyah

Last class at Flamenco Works
at the Central Avenue city studio.
Jesús has lost his voice.
Now Amalyah is the teacher
with her baby Jesús, 8 months old,
tucked in her sling.

You go girl, I think,
you: the wife, the mother,
the dancer, the teacher—
so capable and strong—
the dancemaker
of a new work of art.

7pm—
night rolls out,
the street is humming:
El Rey lowrider Chevy Impala cars;
motorcyclists with skull tattoos;
homeless, some numbing
some feeling their pain;
the young, gliding and oblivious;
the not-so-young, still holding on—
but baby Jesús is falling asleep,
golpe golpe golpe his lullaby.

8pm—
walking back to my car.
I pass a woman particular with her
razor cut hair design.
Still here.

Is she her barber?
Is this street corner her shop?
She is an artist too.

Vibrant red and orange and green. Alive.

This is Life,
like baby Jesús.

I am

por Jesús

I am cleaning the windows
fingerprint free,
grime-free.

I am cleaning the windows of
our dance studio.
Now a clear view.
A fractal of the universe.

Here, my credentials don't matter.
Rank doesn't matter.
Here I dance.
Now I can.
I proudly barter,
no job too lowly.
I clean
for the chance to dance
the Flamenco.

My Alma
directs my cleaning performance
from the studio rocking chair.
Bravo, Mama!
Bravo!

Jesús, my teacher, peeks in.
Hola, ¿que tal?
He speaks to me,
      his cleaner
      his pupil
      his friend.

Duende

Once I knew the muse.

Downpour of ideas,
flood of dreams,
ocean of words...

I could not find—or conceive of—
a bucket big enough
to contain them all!

I LIVED *duende*.

~~~~8/28/15~~~~

The day the spigot shut off.

Dryness

Barrenness

Incomprehensibleness

For a long time, empty bucket.

Where are you, muse?

I twist the handle.

Just drops.

My muse
used to seek me out—*tackle* me!

Now I
search for *duende*.

I still take my pen
into my now-numb fingers
trying to coax my words out

but the pen doesn't move
fast enough to express
the torrent of my emotion.

Nor yet my feet (*golpe! golpe! golpe!*).

But I practice. I work hard.

And I have hope
for both.

Gratitude

Deep gratitude to my huge-hearted husband, Nick, for his patience and love, and for supporting me as I struggle and pursue my new dreams. And to Alma, my daughter, my spark and joy.

To my dear family: Mom, Dad, Katrina, Cam, and Eric. Thank you for your everlasting support on this often very difficult journey. And a special thank you to Emily Grace, my sister, my friend, and warrior.

To Aunt Claudia and Badiah. I love you and treasure the wonderful memories we've made through the years.

To Uncle Hark and Peggy, Uncle Rob and Mardel, Claire, Adam, Paul, and RJ. I love you and am proud to be family with you.

And to my extended family: Dean, Jerime, Susie, Michael, Annalee, Virginia, and Paul. You brighten my life with your presence.

Special thanks for the rare gift of words and generosity: Rob Grant, brother-in-law and editor, and Jasen Christensen, friend and editor. And to Katjriana Hervey, sister-in-law and graphic designer, and Jeremy Warren, friend and graphic designer: I so appreciate you and your help!

Thank you, Gabby Giffords, for your thoughtful and powerful foreword. So kind of you! Thanks also to Nassim Assefi, Juhi Bansal, Lauren Camp, PW Covington, Fabi Hirsch Kruse, Paulann Petersen, and Kim Stafford for reading my manuscript and saying such generous and encouraging things about it. Kindness compounded!

Profound thanks to the following friends for helping me find my way: Rach, Rasha, Linda, Christina S, Laura, Amber, Gina, Emily W, Karen A, Denise, Janelle & Brad, Lyndall, Beth, Barb, Robert, Lars, Paula & Scott, Dorothy, Ragad, Nour, Tigist, Hilary, Suzanne, Atifa, Julie, Amy, Clydette, the Plog Family, Paul, Christina HD, Carolina, Pamela, Jenny, Natalie, Magdy, Artha, Dom, Mel, Susie, Peas, Gabe, Dustin, Megan, Erin, Raushan, Charlie, Mary Ann, Anna S, Amena, Sirena, Jessie, Kait, Meg, Nadia, Emily F, Shaynor, Krysta, Kaitlyn, Catherine, Karen R, Michelle, Friends of Aphasia: Tucson, AZ, Co-Housing ABQ community, and friends in Punta Arenas, Chile.

To my friends with ties to Afghanistan: Aman, Wahid, Timur, Zarifa, Khujesta, Mahtab, Somaia, Elaha, Annika, Aria, Omaid & Lima, Shafie, Samir, Fazelhaq, Rohullah, Farid, Shaharzad, Noorjahan, Abdul Waheed, Jebrael, Haqmal, Said Agha, Ahmadullah, Amina, Nahid, Karen C, Katrina & Curt, Ruchi, Don, Dave B, the Rustaqi Family, the Tanin Family, and Mule Train Rescue. *Tashakur bisyar ziyad!*

And I cannot express enough thanks to Anne Foley: patient, caring, and insightful Writing Coach. We tackled this together!

I am also indebted to the following dear people who have so resolutely walked alongside me: Juhi Bansal, Composer, Conductor, and Teacher; Jocelyn Hagen, Composer, Performer, and Speaker; Steve Myland, Songwriter, Singer, and Musician; Daniela Zormeier, Music Therapist; Molly Wingate, Poetry Therapist; Julianna Tibbet & Robin

Mirante, Speech-Language Pathologists; Fabi Hirsch Kruse, Speech-Language Pathologist; Jesús and Amalyah Muñoz, Flamenco Dancers, Artists, and Maestro y Maestra; Andrea Lozano, Kayla Lyall, and Rina Orellana, Flamenco Dancers, Artists, and Maestras; Kristy Cordova, Jamee Richardson, and Jacque Penunuri, Community Care Specialists; Kamran Talattof, Professor & Mentor, Persian Literature; Layla Hudson, Professor, Gender & Women's Studies; Susan Briante, Professor, Creative Writing; Anne Betteridge, Professor, Anthropology.

I wish also to acknowledge the incredible support I have received from the following organizations: Pat Tillman Foundation, Wounded Warrior Project, and Neuro Community Care (NCC).

And to my readers: Thank you for receiving and trusting my words.

No doubt I have inadvertently omitted the names of people who are dear to me and deserve recognition as well. My sincere apologies! (I blame aphasia.)

Sources I Have Drawn Strength From

Ackerman, Diane. *One Hundred Names for Love: A Stroke, a Marriage, and the Language of Healing.* W. W. Norton & Company, 2011.

Chang, Victoria. *Obit.* Copper Canyon Press, 2020.

Cohen, Nan. *Thousand-Year-Old Words.* Glass Lyre Press, 2021.

Cousineau, Phil. *Once and Future Myths: The Power of Ancient Stories in Modern Times.* Conari Press, 2001.

Doidge, Norman. *The Brain That Changes Itself: Stories of Personal Triumph from the Frontiers of Brain Science.* Penguin Life, 2010.

Giffords, Gabrielle & Kelly, Mark. *Gabby: A Story of Courage, Love, and Resilience.* Scribner, 2011.

Greig, Pete. *God on Mute: Engaging the Silence of Unanswered Prayer.* Regal Books, 2007.

Loorz, Victoria. *Church of the Wild: How Nature Invites Us into the Sacred.* Broadleaf Books, 2021.

McGuire, Dawn. *The Aphasia Café.* IF SF Publishing, 2012.

Sacks, Oliver. *Musicophilia: Tales of Music and the Brain.* Vintage, 2008.

Schwartz, M.D., Jeffrey M., and Begley, Sharon. *The Mind &
The Brain: Neuroplasticity and the Power of Mental Force.*
Harper Perennial, 2002.

Stafford, Kim. *Circumference: Poems of Consolation & Blessing.*
Little Infinities, 2017.

Wooldridge, Susan G. *poemcrazy: freeing your life with words.*
Three Rivers Press, 1996.

About the Author

Farzana Marie is a poet, writer, artist, and stroke survivor.

She received her PhD from the University of Arizona, with a focus on Persian Literature and a minor in Creative Writing. She also has an MA in English Literature from the University of Massachusetts Boston and a BS in Humanities from the US Air Force Academy. Her poetry and translations have appeared in numerous print and online journals.

Farzana served on active duty in the US Air Force for ten years, including two consecutive years deployed in Afghanistan (where she previously also served as a civilian volunteer at a Kabul orphanage).

Presently, she is in the planning phase of The Soul of Language Museum, an immersive multi-sensory experience, to be located in New Mexico, where she lives with her husband and daughter. She is also writing her memoir.

More at: www.farzanamarie.com